Animals

Les animaux

lezanee-*moh*

Illustrated by Clare Beaton

Illustré par Clare Beaton

b small publishing

cat

le chat

ler shah

dog

le chien

ler shee-*yah*

horse

le cheval

ler sh-*val*

COW

la vache

lah vash

rabbit

le lapin

ler lap-*pah*

sheep

le mouton

ler moo-*toh*

goat

la chèvre

lah shevr'

chicken

le poulet

ler poo-*leh*

mouse

la souris

lah soo-*ree*

pig

le cochon

ler coh-*shoh*

duck

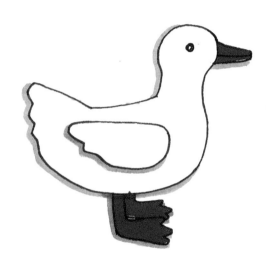

le canard

ler can-*ar*

A simple guide to pronouncing the French words

- Read this guide as naturally as possible, as if it were British English of a generally South-Eastern variety (so-called RP).
- Put stress on the letters in *italics* e.g. lombool-*onss*.
- Don't roll the r at the end of the word, for example in the French word le (the): ler.

Les animaux	lezanee-*moh*	**Animals**
le chat	ler shah	**cat**
le chien	ler shee-*yah*	**dog**
le cheval	ler sh-*val*	**horse**
la vache	lah vash	**cow**
le lapin	ler lap-*pah*	**rabbit**
le mouton	ler moo-*toh*	**sheep**
la chèvre	lah shevr'	**goat**
le poulet	ler poo-*leh*	**chicken**
la souris	lah soo-*ree*	**mouse**
le cochon	ler coh-*shoh*	**pig**
le canard	ler can-*ar*	**duck**

Published by b small publishing
The Book Shed, 36 Leyborne Park, Kew, Richmond, Surrey, TW9 3HA, UK
www.bsmall.co.uk
© b small publishing, 1994 and 2008 (new cover)
4 5 6
All rights reserved.
Printed in China by WKT Company Ltd.
ISBN-13: 978-1-874735-80-9 (UK paperback)
Cataloguing-in-Publication Data:
A catalogue record for this book is available from the British Library